Fan's Dictionary – Sou
Songbook

Over the years Southampton F.C. fans have created incredible atmospheres in football grounds and come up with some of the creative chants and songs. This book is a guide for these chants and songs written by the Southampton F.C. supporters. From the When the Saints Go Marching In, We All Follow Southampton, Southampton Boys, Pompey Fan on a String, All Southampton, When I Was Just a Little Boy, to songs dedicated to the various players and staff, the very best of the terrace chants, songs, and timeless classics, this book will delight and entertain in equal measure and honors every single Southampton F.C. fan who has ever sung in support for the team throughout its proud history.

All the songs and chants in this book are written and sang by the Southampton F.C. supporters during football matches, at pubs and bars or posted to message boards, they are not the thoughts or views of the authors.

WRITE TO US

We greatly value your opinion. We would love to hear your thoughts and recommendations about this book so we can improve! Write to us: fansdictionary@gmail.com

COPYRIGHT

Copyright © 2020 by Fan's Dictionary

The author have provided this book to you for your personal use only. Thank you for buying and for complying with copyright laws by not reproducing, scanning, or distributing any part of it in any form without permission.

ADAM LALLANA

He plays on the left,
He plays on the right,
Adam Lallana,
Makes Messi look s*ite...

ADAM LALLANA 2

Viva Lallana,
Viva Lallana,
Runnin' down the wing,
Hear Southampton sing,
Viva Lallana...

ADAM LALLANA 3

He's off to Brazil,
He's off to Brazil,
Adam Lallana,
He's off to Brazil...

ALAN PARDEW'S RED ARMY

Alan Pardew's red army,
Alan Pardew's red army,
Alan Pardew's red army...

ALEX CHAMBERLAIN

Na na na na na na na na na na na,
Alex Chamberlain,
Chamberlain,
Chamberlain,
Alex Chamberlain.

ALL SOUTHAMPTON

And it's all Southampton,
All Southampton FC,
We're by far the greatest team,
The world has ever seen...

ALWAYS LOOK ON THE BLUE SIDE FOR SH*TE

Always look on the blue side for sh*te,
Da da-da da-da da-da da-da...
Always look on the blue side for sh*te,
Da da-da da-da da-da da-da.

ALWAYS RUNNING

Tottenham always running,
Arsenal running too,
Southamptons always running,
Running after you.

ANDREW SURMAN

You are our Surman, our Andrew Surman,
You scored a hatrick last year at home,
You'll never know Drew,
How much we love you,
Chelsea leave our Surman alone.

ANTTI NIEMI

Ohhhh Antti Niemi came down from hearts one night,
Oh Antti Niemi saved every shot in sight on,
Antti Niemi we're all right behind yooouuu.

ARE YOU WATCHING POMPEY SCUM

Are you watching are you watching,
Are you watching Pompey scum,
Are you watching Pompey scum?

BACK OF MILTON ROAD

We all live in the back of Milton Road,
The back of Milton road,
We all live in the back of Milton Road,
The back of Milton road...

BIG CLUB

Big club,
You used to be a big club,
You used to be a big club,
You used to be a big club...

BILLY SHARP

Ole ole ole ole,
Ole ole ole ole,
Billy Sharp Sharp Sharp...

BRADLEY WRIGHT-PHILIPS

He robs from the Skates,
He robs from the Skates,
Bradley Wright-Philips,
He robs from the Skates...

BUILD A BONFIRE

Build a bonfire,
Build a bonfire,
Stick Pompey on the top,
Tottenham Hotspur in the middle,
And then burn the f***ing lot.

BUILD IT UP WITH RED AND WHITE

Build it up with Red and White,
Red and White, Red and White,
Build it up with Red and White,
Poor old Pompey.

BYE BYE POMPEY

Bye, bye Pompey,
Pompey, bye bye,
Bye, bye Pompey,
Pompey, bye bye...

CEDRIC SOARES

He's our Cedric,
Running down the wing he's electric,
He's done things we never expected,
And shits on clyne.

CEDRIC SOARES 2

He's our Cedric,
Running down the wing he's electric,
He's done things I never expected,
and I need more time.

CHARLIE AUSTIN

Charlie Austin's red and white,
Red and white, red and white,
Charlie Austin's red and white,
He hates Pompey.

CHARLIE AUSTIN 2

We say that we love you,
(Say that we love you),
Say that we need you,
(Say that we need you).

We've got Charlie Austin,
We've got,
Charlie Austin,
We've got,
Charlie Austin,
He scores goals, goals, goals.

CHARLIE WAYMAN

Up the middle for Charlie,
Down the middle he'll run,
Up the middle for Charlie,
He'll score the goals for fun.

CLAUS LUNDEKVAM

Our Claus in the middle of defence,
Our Claus in the middle of defence,
Our Claus in the middle of defence,
Our Claus in the middle of defence...

COME ON YOU REDS

Come on you reds,
Come on you reds,
Come on you reds,
Come on...

DANNY INGS

Danny Ings is the king I say,
Danny Ings is the king of the scummers,
Smashing Pompey the Southampton way...

DANNY INGS 2

There's something that the Saints want you
to know,
The best in the world he is one of our own,
Our number nine,
Give him the ball he will score every time,
Si senor,
Give the ball to Danny and he will score.

DEJAN LOVREN

F**k off Lovren,
Dejan Lovren,
We just don't want you anymore,
Your wife showed you the door,
You money grabbing w**re,
Please just f**k off Lovren.

DEJAN LOVREN 2

Ayyyyyyy,
Dejan Lovren,
Uhhhh ahhh,
I wanna knowwwww,
Why your such a c**t...

DER F*CK OFF

Der
Der der,
Der der, der der, der der,
Der der, der dede der,
Der de der der der de, de.....
F*ck off.

DIRTY NORTHERNERS

You dirty northern b*stards,
You dirty northern b*stards,
You dirty northern b*stards...

DUSAN TADIC

He plays on the left,
He plays on the right,
Dusan Tadic makes Lallana look s*ite,
S*ite, s*ite, s*ite.

DUSAN TADIC 2

Woa-oah, woa-oah,
Du-san Tad-ic,
Woa-oah, woa-oah,
Du-san Tad-ic.

DUSAN TADIC 3

Go on, go on Dusan Taaadic,
Go on, go on Dusan Taaadic,
Go on, go on Dusan Taaadic,
Go on, go on Dusan Taaadic...

EIEIEIO

Eeeeh I eeh I eeh I oh,
Up the football league we go,
And when we get to the play offs,
This is what we'll sing,
We're Southampton,
Super Southampton,
Pardew is our king.

EMPTY SEATS

They're here,
They're there,
They're every f*ckin where,
Empty seats, empty seats...

FRATTON PARK IS FALLIN DOWN

Fratton Park is fallin down,
Falin down fallin down,
Fratton Park is fallin down poor old Pompey,
Build it up in Red and White,
Red and White Red and White,
Build it up in Red and White poor old
pompey,

We hate Pompey,
We hate Pompey...

FRATTON PARK IS NEVER FULL

Ohh Fratton Park,
Ohh Fratton Park,
Is never full,
Is never full,
Unless they play Southampton,
Ohh Fratton Park is never full...

GARETH BALE

Baaaale, wherever you may be,
You s*ag sheep in your own country,
It could be worse,
Cause you could be a skate,
And take your own sister out on a date.

GASTON RAMIREZ

Gaston Ramirez,
Gaston Ramirez,
Comes from Italy f****n hates Pompy,
Gaston Ramirez.

GASTON RAMIREZ 2

Gaston,
Gaston Ramirez runs down the wing for me,
Da da da da da.

GEORGE BURLEY'S RED ARMY

George Burley's red army,
We hate Pompey,
George Burley's red army,
We hate Pompey,
George Burley's red army,
We hate Pompey,
George Burley's red army,
We hate Pompey...

GORDON RAMSEY FOR NORWICH

There's Only One Gordon Ramsey,
There's Only One Gordon Ramsey,
One Gordon Ramsey,
Ooohhh Theres Only One Gordon Ramsey...

GRAZIANO PELLE

Graziano, da da da-da-da,
Graziano, da da da-da-da,
Graziano, da da da-da-da...

GRAZIANO PELLE 2

Come to see Pelle,
You've only come to see Pelle,
Come to see Pelle,
You've only come to see Pelle.

GRAZIANO PELLE 3

Grazziano Pele's
A lovely looking fella,
His hair is full of lacker,
Southampton's goal Machine.

GRAZIANO PELLE 4

Everybody loves him,
Everybody wants him,
To play for their team,
But he won't go, he is our hero,
Our Italian number nine.

GRZEGORZ RASIAK

Na na na na na na na na Gregorz Rasiak,
Rasiak, Gregorz Rasiak,
Na na na na na na na na Gregorz Rasiak,
Rasiak, Gregorz Rasiak.

GULY

Ole, ole, ole, ole,
Guly, Guly,
Ole, ole, ole, ole,
Guly, Guly...

HARRY REDKNAPP

Harry Redknapp's got a twitch ei ei o,
With a twitch twitch here,
And a twitch twitch there,
Here a twitch,
There a twitch,
Everywhere a twitch twitch,
Harry Redknapp's got a twitch ei ei o.

HARRY REDKNAPP 2

Who the f*ck is Harry Redknapp,
Who the f*ck is Harry Redknapp,
Who the f*ck is Harry Redknapp,
When the Saints go marching,
On,
On,
On.

HELLO WE ARE SOUTHAMPTON BOYS

Hello hello, hello hello,
We are the Southampton boys,
Hello hello,
We are the Southampton boys,
And if you are a Portsmouth fan,
Surrender or you'll die,
We all follow Southampton.

HELLO WE ARE SOUTHAMPTON BOYS 2

Hello hello, hello hello,
We are Southampton Boys,
Hello hello,
We are Southampton Boys,
And if you are a Pompey fan,
Then you can all f**k off,
We all follow Southampton.

HE'S OUR NUMBER

He's our number 1 he saves with his thumb
Kelvin Kelvin,
He's our number 2 he's got quick feet Frazer
Frazer,
He's our number 3 he's got a good left shoe
Harding Harding,
He's our number 4 he's always on the floor
Morgan Morgan,
He's our number 5 he's never dived Ryan
Ryan,
He's our number 6 he takes no s**t Jose
Jose,
He's our number 7 he came from heaven
Rickie Rickie,
He's our number 9 he's blooming Sublime
Barnard Barnard,
He's our number 10 he's s**t again Jason
Jason...

...He's our number 11 he came fom near heaven Guly Guly,
He's our number 12 he'll have a Delve Danny Danny,
He's our number 20 he gives us plenty Adam Adam
He's our number 30 he plays very dirty Richard Richard...

HOLLOW

Hollow, hollow, hollow,
Pompey's sucess is f*cking hollow,
All that money they took,
From that big russian crook,
And their stadiums still a s***hole.

HOT DOG SAUSAGE

Hot dog sausage roll,
Come on Saints score a goal.

I CAN'T READ AND I CAN'T WRITE

I can't read and I can't write, but that don't
really matter,
I come from down in Southampton town,
and I can drive a tractor.
I can plough, and milk a cow, and drive a big
green mower,
But the thing that I like best is being a
strawberry grower.
Ooooh-aaarrrrrrrrrrrrrr.

I WANNA GO HOME

I wanna go home,
I wanna go home,
Bournemouth's a sh*t hole,
I wanna go home...

IF YOU ALL HATE POMPEY CLAP YOUR HANDS

If you all hate Pompey clap your hands,
(Clap clap),
If you all hate Pompey clap your hands,
(Clap clap),
If you all hate Pompey, all hate Pompey,
If you all hate Pompey clap your hands,
(Clap clap).

IF YOU ARE STANDING ON CORNER

If you're standing on a corner,
With a blue scarf round your neck,
Southampton boys will come and get ya,
And we'll break your f*cking neck.

IN YOUR LIVERPOOL SLUMS

In your Liverpool slums,
In your Liverpool slums,
You look in the dustbin for something to eat,
You find a dead cat and you think it' a treat,
In your Liverpool slums.

IS THERE A FIRE DRILL BOURNEMOUTH

Is there a fire drill,
Is there a fire drill,
Is there a fire drill,
Is there a fire drill...

JAMES WARD-PROWSE

Oh, Prowsey Prowsey,
He's used to be a skate but he's alright now.

JAMES WARD-PROWSE 2

James Ward Prowse,
My lord,
James Ward Prowse,
Oooo James Ward Prowse.

JANNIK VESTERGAARD

Du du du du du du du Jannik Vestergaard,
Du du du du du du du.

JASON PUNCHEON

He went for a s*it,
He went for a s*it,
Jason Puncheon,
He went for a s*it.

He s*its when he wants,
He s*its when he wants,
Jason Puncheon,
He s*its when he wants.

JAY RODRIGUEZ

And it's Jay Rodriguez,
It's Jay Rodriguez,
And he's always scoring goals,
Scoring goals like Jay,
Always does.

JHON VIAFARA

De de der,
Jhon Viafara,
De de der,
Jhon Viafara,
De de der,
Jhon Viafara...

JINGLE BELLS

Jingle bells, jingle bells,
Jingle all the way,
Oh what fun it is to see Southampton win
away,
Hey...

JOSE FONTE

Jose Fonte baby,
Jose Fonte oooohhhh.

KELVIN DAVIES

Super, super, Kelv,
Super, super, Kelv,
Super Kelvin Davies...

LEE BARNARD

Lee Bernard, Bernard,
His shot is pretty f*cking hard,
He's better than Frank Lampard, Lampard,
Oh Lee Barnard, Barnard...

LET'S ALL HAVE A DISCO

Let's all have a disco,
Let's all have a disco,
lalala la,
lalala la,
Let's all have a disco,
Let's all have a disco,
lalala la,
lalala la...

LUKE SHAW

Na, na, na, na, na, Luke Shaw.

MANOLO GABBIADINI

Les Reed went to Europe,
To buy a Lamborghini,
Instead he bought a striker,
His name is Gabbiadini,
He scores goals with his left foot,
He scores goals with his right,
And when he scores another goal,
We'll sing this song all night.
Ohhhhh...

MANOLO GABBIADINI 2

We've got,
(Clap,clap) Gabbiadini,
We've got,
(Clap,clap) Gabbiadini,
We've got,
(Clap,clap) Gabbiadini,
And he scores goals goals and goals.

MAREK SAGANOWSKI

De de de de Saganowski,
De de de de Saganowski,
De de de de Saganowski...

MARIO LEMINA

Ohhhh, Mario Lemina,
Ohhhh,
He's a class midfielder,
Ohhhh,
He never gives the ball away,
1, 2, 3, 4...

MARKUS LIEBHERR

St Markus....we do,
St Markus....we do,
St Markus....weee doooo,
Oh St Markus we love you.

MARKUS LIEBHERR 2

There's only one Markus Liebherr,
Only one Markus Liebherr,
Walking along singing a song,
Walking in a one Liebherr wonder land...

MATT LE TISSIER

Le Tiss, Le Tiss,
Matt Matt Le Tiss,
He get's the ball he takes the p*ss,
Matt Matt Le Tiss...

MATT LE TISSIER 2

Oooooooooon the p*ss, the p*ss, the p*ss,
For Matt Le Tiss, Le Tiss, Le Tiss,
He's the leader of our football team.
He's the greatest, p*ss taker,
That the wooooorld have ever seen...

MAYA YOSHIDA

Maya hee,
Maya haa,
Maya who,
Maya Yoshida.

MAYA YOSHIDA 2

Oh, May-a Yosh-ida,
Oh, May-a Yosh-ida..

MICK CHANNON

Channon here,
Channon there,
Channon every f**kingwhere,
Lalalalalalalalala.

MICKEY EVANS

Hey Mickey you're so fine,
You're so fine you're number 9,
Hey Mickey,
(Clap clap clap),
Hey Mickey.

MORGAN SCHNEIDERLIN

Scores on a Tuesday,
He only scores on a Tuesday,
Scores on a Tuesday,
He only scores on a Tuesday...

MOUSSA DJENEPO

Moussa,
Moussa Djenepo runs down the wing for
me...

MY OLDMAN SAID

My oldman said be a p*mpey fan,
I said f*ck off bollox your a c*nt,
With hatchetts and hammers,
Stanley knives and spanners,
Show the p*mpey b*astards how to fight,
I'd rather s*ag a bucket with a big hole in it
than be a p*ompey fan.

NATHAN REDMOND

Nathan Redmond,
Oh he is so wonderful,
When he scores a goal,
Oh it's beautiful, magical,
When he runs down the wing,
He's as fast as lightning,
It's frightening,
And he makes all the boys sing,
Der der der der der der der.

NATHAN REDMOND 2

Nathan Redmond da da da da da,
Nathan Redmond da da da da da,
Nathan Redmond da da da da da...

NATHAN REDMOND 3

There's a star man,
Playing on the right,
His name is Nathan Redmond,
And he's f*cking dynamite

NICOLA CORTESE

Cortese woah, Cortese woah,
He comes from Italy,
He f*cking hates pompey...

NIGEL ADKINS

E I E I E I O,
Up the football league we go,
When we get promotion
This is what we sing,
We are Southampton, we are Southampton,
Adkins is our king.

OH DEANO

Oh Deano's f**kin' magic,
He wears a magic hat,
And when he saw St Mary's,
He said I fancy that,
He didn't sign for Pomey,
Or Bournemouth 'coz they're sh*te,
He signed for Southampton,
'Coz they're f**king dynamite...

ON THE WELSH SIDE OF THE BRIDGE

Always s*it on the Welsh side of the bridge,
Da do da do de do de do,
Always s*it on the Welsh side of the bridge,
Da do da do de do de do...

ONE TEAM IN HAMPSHIRE

One team in Hampshire,
There's only one team in Hampshire,
One team in Hampshire,
There's only one team in Hampshire...

ORIOL ROMEU

Ori-oriol,
Ori-oriol,
Oriol Romeu,
Ori-oriol,
Ori-oriol,
Oriol Romeu,
Ori-oriol,
Ori-oriol,
Oriol Romeu.

PHIL THOMPSON

Sit down Pinocchio,
Sit down Pinocchio.

PIERRE HOJBJERG

Ohhhh, Pierre Hojbjerg,
One and only,
They said that he was finished if he stayed in
Germany,
But now he's on the south coast,
And he fucking hates Pompey,
Ohhhh...

POMPEY GOT BATTERED

1-2-3-4,
Pompey got battered,
4-0 at home,
Pompey got battered,
4-0 at home,
4-0 at hoooome...

POMPEY'S GOING DOWN

They're going down,
They're going down,
They're going down,
Pompey's going down with no money in the bank,
No money in the bank.
Pompey's going down with no money in the bank,
No money in the bank,
No money in the bank...

...They're going down,
They're going down,
Going doooown,
Going doooown...

Going doooowwwwn,
Going doooowwwwn...

PORTSMOUTH IS FULL SH*T

Oh Portsmouth is full of sh*t,
It's full of sh*t, sh*t and more sh*t,
Oh Portsmouth is full of s**t...

QUE SERA SERA

Tell yer ma, yer ma,
You won't be home for tea,
The Saints are at Wembley
Que sera sera...

RADHI JAÏDI

Jaidi whoa,
Jaidi whoaaaaaa,
He comes from Tunisia,
He'll f*ckin murder you...

RALPH HASENHÜTTL

This is how it feels to be Pompey,
This is how it feels to be small,
You sign Jackett,
We sign Hasenhüttl, Hasenhüttl.

RED ARMY

Red army,
Red army,
Red army,
Red army,
Red army...

RED N WHITE

Red n white, Barmy army,
Red n white, Barmy army,
Red n white, Barmy army...

REFEREE YOU DON'T KNOW WHAT YOU'RE DOING

You don't know what you're doing,
You don't know what you're doing,
You don't know what you're doing...

RICHARD CHAPLOW

Der der der der der Richard Chaplow der der der der,
Der der der der der Richard Chaplow der der der der,
Der der der der der Richard Chaplow der der der der...

RICHARD CHAPLOW 2

He playes on the Left, centre mid,
That boy Richard Chaplow,
Could play for Madrid.

RICKIE LAMBERT

He stands just over six-foot-three,
Rickie, Rickie,
He'll take us to the Premier League,
Rickie, Rickie,
He gets the ball he takes the p*ss,
He wears the shirt of Matt Le Tiss,
Rickie Lambert, Southampton's goal
machine.
La la la la la la la la, la la, la la,
La la la la la la la la, la la, la la,
La la la la la la la la, la la la la la la la la,
Rickie Lambert, Southampton's goal
machine!

RICKIE LAMBERT 2

Rickie Lambert score more goals,
Rickie lambert score more goals...

RICKIE LAMBERT 3

Oh Rickie you're so fine,
You're so fine,
You blow our minds,
Score Rickie.

RUDI SKACEL

Rudi, Rudi, Rudi,
Rudi, Rudi,
Skacel,
Rudi, Rudi, Rudi,
Rudi, Rudi,
Skacel...

RUPERT LOWE

Swing Lowe,
Swing Rupert Lowe,
Swing him from Itchin Bridge...

Swing Lowe,
Swing Rupert Lowe,
Swing him from Itchin Bridge...

RYAN BERTRAND

Step inside here comes the pace,
Take that look from off your face,
You ain't catching Ry Bertrand nowwww.

SADIO MANE

Step inside here comes the pace,
Take that look from off your face,
You ain't catching Sadio nowwww.

Ooooh Sadio Mane,
You know it's too late as he's running on by,
Ooooh Sadio Mane,
But don't look back in anger, he's scored
again.

SAINTS ARE GOING UP

Saints are going up,
Saints are going up,
And now your gonna beleive us,
And now your gonna beleive us,
And now your gonna beleive uuussssss,
Cus Saints are going up.

SAINTS WILL TEAR YOU APART AGAIN

Saints saints will tear you apart,
Again,
Saints saints will tear you apart,
Again...

SHALL WE SING A SONG FOR YOU

Shall we sing,
Shall we sing,
Shall we sing a song for you,
Shall we sing a song for you...

SHANE LONG

Laaaaa,
La, la, la-la-la-la,
Shane Long
Shane Long...

SHANE LONG 2

Shane long, super Shane long,
He's our super Irish goal machine,
From the Emerald Isles,
He's the best they've had since Robbie
Keane.

SHOW THEM THE WAY TO GO HOME

Show them the way to go home,
They're tired and they want to go to bed,
Coz there's only half a football team,
Compared to the boys in,
Red and white stripes,
Black shorts,
Red socks with a white hoop round the top.
Hey!

SING WHEN YOU ARE WINNING

Sing when you're winning,
You only sing when you're winning,
Sing when you're winning,
You only sing when you're winning...

SIT DOWN IF YOU'RE A POMPEY FAN

Sit down if you're a Pompey fan,
Sit down if you're a Pompey fan,
Sit down if you're a Pompey fan,
Sit down if you're a Pompey fan.

SIT DOWN SHUT UP

Sit down shut up,
Sit down shut up,
Sit down shut up,
Sit down shut up...

SOFIANE BOUFAL

Where it began,
I cant begin to knowing,
But then I know we're growing strong,
Was in the spring,
The spring became the summer,
Who'd have believed you come along,
Fans, touching fans,
Reaching out, touching me, touching you,
Sofiane Boufal, oh oh oh,
Football's never looked so good,
Im mezmorized, oh oh oh,
When the ball is at your foot,
Oh oh oh.

SOFIANE BOUFAL 2

Ole, ole ole ole,
Bou-fal,
Bou-fal...

SOUTHAMPTON LALA

Southampton lala,
Southampton lala,
Southampton lala,
Southampton lala...

SOUTHAMPTON ARE THE GREATEST

Oooooh what's the team we all love best,
Southampton are the greatest,
The special team that can beat the rest,
Southampton are the greatest,
Watch them play in pub or club or any place,
Southampton are the greatest.

SOUTHAMPTON BOYS ARE IN TOWN

We are the southampton,
The pride of the south,
We hate all them b*stards,
That come from Portsmouth,
They only drink Cresta,
They only drink Coke,
The Pompey boys are a joke,
La la la, la la la la la,
We only drink whisky,
We only drink brown,
The southampton boys are in town.

SOUTHAMPTON CLAP

Southampton, (clap clap, clap),
Southampton, (clap clap, clap),
Southampton, (clap clap, clap),
Southampton, (clap clap, clap)...

SOUTHAMPTON TILL I DIE

Southampton till I die,
I'm Southampton till I die,
I know I am I'm sure I am,
I'm Southampton till I die...

SOUTHAMPTON TILL I DIE 2

I'm southampton till I die,
You're Portsmouth till july,
We're going up,
You're going down,
So f**k off and goodbye...

SOUTHAMPTON'S BACK FOUR

Ryan Bertrand, he is our left back,
Virgil Van DiJk beside him,
Cedric and Jose Fonte
Southampton's back four...

...You know no one can beat them,
You know you can't defeat them,
They're just too f*****g awesome,
Southampton's back four.

SOUTHERNERS

Southerners,
Southerners,
Southerners,
Southerners,
Southerners,
Southerners,
Southerners...

STAND UP IF YOU LOVE THE SAINTS

Stand up if you love the Saints,
Stand up if you love the Saints,
Stand up if you love the Saints,
Stand up if you love the Saints...

STERN JOHN

Stern John,
Terrorizing the defence,
Stern John,
Terrorizing the defence...

STEVEN DAVIS

You are my Davis, my Stevie Davis,
You make me happy when skies are gray,
So f**k your Lampard and Stevie Gerrard,
But please don't take my Davis away.

STILL GOT GULY ON THE BENCH

We still got Guly on the bench,
And we still got Guly on the bench,
Still got Guly,
Still got Guly on the bench...

STUART ARMSTRONG

When Celtic rang,
We know we found the right Scottish man,
Ooh words can't describe,
When he's playing in the red and white.

His hair is fine,
He scores belters all the time,
That's why we sing this song,
For Stuart Armstrong
Do do do do.

TADANARI LEE

Tadanari Lee,
Tadanari Lee,
Hot him on a free,
And he eat sushi,
Tadanari Lee...

THAT'S WHAT IT'S LIKE TO BE POMPEY

That's what it's like to be Pompey,
That's what it's like to be poor,
You signed Whittingham,
We signed Pochettino,
Pochettino, Pochettino...

THE POMPEY FAMILY

Your father is your brother,
Your sister is your mother,
You all s**g one another,
The Pompey family...

THE SAINTS

(Claps)
The Saints,
(Claps)
The Saints..

THE SOUTH COAST IS OURS

The South Coast is ours,
The South Coast is ours,
We are Southampton,
The South Coast is ours...

THE STANDS

Northam stand:
We're the Northam we're the Northam we're the Northam over here.

Kingsland stand:
We're the Kingsland we're the Kingsland we're the Kingsland over here.

Itchen stand:
We're the Itchen we're the Itchen we're the Itchen over here.

Chapel Stand: Sssshhhhh.

TOP OF THE LEAGUE

Top of the league you're having a laugh,
Top of the league you're having a laugh,
Top of the league you're having a laugh...

VICTOR WANYAMA

It's Wanyama,
Victor Wanyama,
Wanyama, Wanyama, woah...

VICTOR WANYAMA 2

He's a Kenyan, a mighty Kenyan, called
Victor Wanyama,
He's a Kenyan, a mighty Kenyan, called
Victor Wanyama,
A Wanyama, a Wanyama, a Wanyama...

VIRGIL VAN DIJK

We've got Van Dijk, Virgil Van Dijk,
I just don't think you understand,
He's Clude Puels man,
He's better than Zidane,
We've got Virgil Van Dijk.

VIRGIL VAN DIJK 2

When I'm with you Virgil,
I go out of my head,
And I just can't get enough,
And I just can't get enough,
All the things you do for me,
And everything you said,
I just can't get enough,
I just can't get enough,
We slip and slide as we fall in love,
And I just can't seem to get enough of you,
Du du du du du du,
Du du du du du du,
Du du du du du du,
Virgil Van Dijk.

VIRGIL VAN DIJK 3

We Hate Van Dijk,
Virgin Van Dijk,
You just don't seem to understand,
He's a greedy f*****g snake,
Send him a bomb in a cake,
We hate Van Dijk.

WE ALL FOLLOW SOUTHAMPTON

We all follow Southampton,
Over Land and Sea,
(And Portsmouth),
We all follow Southampton,
Onto Victory,
(Altogether now).

We all follow Southampton,
The Greatest Football Team,
(Not Portsmouth),
We all follow Southampton,
Onto Victory.

WE ALL HATE F*****G POMPEY

We all hate the Pompey boys,
We all hate the Pompey boys,
We all hate the Pompey boys...

WE ARE GOING UP

We are going up, said we are going up,
We are going up, said we are going up,
We are going up, said we are going up...

WE ARE RED WE ARE WHITE

We are red, we are white,
We are f***in dynamite,
La la la la,
La la la,
Lal laaaa.

WE ARE RED YOU ARE BLUE

We are red, you are blue,
We hate pompey through and through,
With a nick nack paddy whack give a skate a slap,
F*ck off Pompey you are crap...

WE ARE SOUTHAMPTON

We are Southampton,
We are Premier League,
We are Premier League,
We are Premier League,
We are Southampton
We are Premier League.

WE ARE SOUTHAMPTON WE ARE THE BEST

We are Southampton, we are the best,
We hate United and we hate the rest,
La la la la, la la la la, la la la-la-la laaaaa.

WE ARE WHITE WE ARE RED

We are white, we are red,
We are mental in the head,
La la la la, la la la, lal laaaa.

WE DON'T CARE ABOUT YOU

We don't care about you,
We don't care about youuuuu,
We are Southampton,
We don't care about you...

WE FORGOT THAT YOU WERE HERE

We forgot,
We forgot,
We forgot that you were here,
We forgot that you were here...

WE HAD JOY WE HAD FUN

We had joy,
We had fun,
We had Pompey on the run,
But the joy didn't last,
Cos the b*stards ran too fast...

WE HATE

We hate Arsenal,
We hate Liverpool too,
We hate West Ham United,
But Southampton we love you...

WE KNOW WE ARE

We're s**t,
And we know we are,
We're s**t,
And we know we are.

WE LOOK DOWN ON THEM

We look down on them in League one,
We won 4-0 and made them run,
Hasenhüttl keeps us going,
And Ings is scoring goals for fun,
Ohhh ohh oh ohhh.

WE LOVE SOUTHAMPTON

We love Southampton, we do,
We love Southampton, we do,
We love Southampton, we do,
Oh Southampton we love you...

WE WANT RUPERT OUT

We want Rupert out,
Say we want Rupert out.

WE'RE STAYING UP

They're staying doooooown,
We're staying uuuuuup,
They're staying doooooown,
Saints are staying up and the skates are
staying down,
The skates are staying down,
The skates are staying down.

WE'VE GOT YOUR BACK FOUR

We've got your back four,
We've got your back four
Who needs Rodriguez,
We've got your back four.

WE'LL DO WHAT WE WANT

We'll do what we want,
We'll do what we wannnnttt,
We are Southampton,
We'll do what we want.

WE'RE COMING FOR YOU

We're coming for you,
We're coming for yoooooooooou,
You dirty Skate b*stards,
We're coming for you...

WE'RE GONNA WIN THE LEAGUE

We're gonna win the league,
We're gonna win the league,
And now you're gonna believe us,
And now you're gonna believe us,
And now you're gonna believe us,
We're gonna win the league.

WE'RE SOUTHAMPTON

We are Southampton,
We are Southampton,
We are Southampton from the Dell,
We are Southampton,
Super Southampton,
We are Southampton from the Dell...

WE'RE TAKING THE P*SS

We're taking the p*ss, we're taking the p*ss,
We are Southampton, we're taking the p*ss...

WHEN I WAS JUST A LITTLE BOY

When I was just a little boy,
My father bought me a favorite toy,
A Pompey fan on a string,
He told me to kick his f*****g head in,
His f*****g head in, his f*****g head in,
He told me to kick his f*****g head in.

When I was just a little boy,
My granddad bought me a favorite toy,
A Pompey fan on a string,
He told me to kick his f*****g head in,
His f*****g head in, his f*****g head in,
He told me to kick his f*****g head in...

WHEN I WAS JUST A LITTLE BOY 2

When I was just a little boy,
I asked my mother what should I be,
Should I be Pompey, should I be Saints,
Here's what she said to me,
Wash your mouth out son,
And go get your father's gun,
And shoot the Pompey scum,
And support the saints,
We hate Pompey, we hate Pompey.

WHEN THE SAINTS GO MARCHING IN

Oh when the Saints, oh when the Saints,
Go marching in, go marching in,
Oh when the Saints go marching in,
I want to be in that number,
Oh when the Saints go marching in...

WHEN YOU WALK DOWN WEMBLEY WAY

When you walk down Wembley Way,
You will hear the Saints say,
We're gonna stuff,
Forest and Brian Clough.

WHO THE F*UCK ARE MAN UTD

Who the f*uck are Man United,
Who the f*uck are Man United,
Who the f*uck are Man United,
And the Saints go marchin on on on.

WHO'S LAUGHING NOW

Tralalalala,
Tralalalalalala,
Tralalalalala,
Who the f*ck is laughing now?

WHO'S THAT TEAM WE CALL SOUTHAMPTON

Who's that team we call Southampton,
Who's that team we all adore,
They're the boys in Red & White,
And their f*cking dynamite
And they're gonna show the bast*rds how to score...

WINGS OF A SPARROW

If I had the wings of a sparrow,
And I had the ass of a crow,
I would fly over Fratton tomorrow,
And S*it on the b*stards below,
Below,
S*it on,
S*it on,
S*it on the b*stards below...

WOOLSTON FERRY

Ohhh the woolston ferry,
It don't travel very fast,
It wasn't built for comfort,
It was built to laaaaaaaaastt.

YELLOWS

Yellows,
Yellows,
Yellows...

YOU LIVE IN A SH*THOLE

You f*ckin live in a s*ithole,
Live in a s*ithole,
You f*ckin live in a s*ithole,
Live in a s*ithole...

YOUR GROUND'S TOO BIG

Your ground's too big for you,
Your ground's too big for you,
Your ground's too big for you,
Your ground's too big for you,
Your ground's too big for you...

YOUR SUPPORT

Your support is,
Your support is,
Your support is f*cking s*it,
Your support is f*cking s*it...

YOU'RE NOT AS GOOD AS US

You're not as good as us,
No,
You're not as good as us,
No,
You're not as good as us,
No,
And you smell like fish.

YOU'RE NOT FIT TO REFEREE

You're not fit to,
You're not fit to,
You're not fit to referee,
You're not fit to referee.

YOU'RE SUPPOSED TO BE AT HOME

You're supposed,
You're supposed,
You're supposed to be at home,
You're supposed to be at home..

Printed in Great Britain
by Amazon

73772308R00058